Copyright © Power Retailing, Inc. All Rights Reserved.

ISBN-13: 978-1511766487

ISBN-10: 1511766484
Published by POWER Retailing, Phoenix, AZ

Printed in the United States of America.

Foreword

This book, *The Ultimate Store Closing Strategy*, is packed with cutting-edge concepts to maximize sales and open your mind to new ideas.

Its sole purpose is to give insights, inspirations, and dozens of strategic ideas to make a successful switch in your life and solve your biggest business challenge.

To multiply your results while reducing your time, effort and risk, wouldn't you like to learn the biggest sales & marketing mistakes that 90% of retailers make and how you can avoid them? Or discover how you can profit during these fast-changing times?

Because every store is unique with different challenges and goals, this illustrated book is NOT written to be a self-promoting sales presentation, an easy how-to recipe, or do-it-yourself manual. It is a guidebook to inform, motivate and encourage you to unlock the hidden wealth in your business, and at the same time take the stress and frustration off your shoulders.

After reading a few pages of this book, some people might say: "There's nothing new here, I already know this stuff. It's common knowledge among us experts."

With all due respect, almost every business with which I have consulted is guilty of major marketing mistakes and the failure of not having a well-organized exit strategy: the best timing, how to advertise, pricing merchandise, when to take reductions, how to create urgency and what strategies will work best for your store, etc.

To stop feeling trapped and to avoid the guesswork, you'll discover an entirely fresh, new way of marketing that may seem like it should have been obvious – but wasn't – until it was revealed to you. Eliminating just one or two of the most common errors can catapult your sales and profits beyond your expectations.

That's why POWER Retailing's comprehensive sure-fire system means faster results and more cash flow than with any other company at any price. And, it can be applied to almost any type of retail store and make your cash registers ring NOW!

By taking action, as an added FREE Bonus you'll gain private access to our personal coaching programs: Plus, 1-hour FREE consultation and evaluation ($300 value) to achieve your goal.

Special Acknowledgements

I would like to express my gratitude to storeowners who used POWER Retailing's liquidation system. Our time-tested strategies have brought hope... inspiration... and heartfelt thanks from satisfied retailers who far exceeded their goals.

Above all I want to thank my loving wife, Stella who supported and helped in the process of coordinating and editing specific steps. In the course of writing this book, without her input the ingredients and graphics could not have been presented in such a well-organized way.

I would like to thank Mr. Chris McCarty, V.P. of POWER Retailing, who has always gone above and beyond the call of duty. His expertise and abilities are exceptional and his accomplishments are too many to mention. He invests the time and effort to do practical things required to help clients succeed and prosper – and that is when miracles begin to happen.

Thanks to Sheryl Keeme for assisting and handling the completion of the manuscript. Without her knowledge and special expertise, this "one-of-a-kind" book would never have been published and found its way.

Last and not least: Thanks to all those special friends, sales reps., business advisors and retail consultants who have known me over the course of the years and whose names I have failed to mention.

--Bob Nelson, POWER Retailing, Founder and President

Table of Contents

Are You Planning On Closing, Retiring, Quitting Or Selling Your Business?

If you've been trying to sell your business without success, we can help convert your inventory into 100% Cash FAST!

Designed to fit your budget, this integrated liquidation strategy can get results easier and faster than you ever thought possible... Without contests, paying extended sales fees and long-term contracts.

Introduction

POWER Retailing

My name is Bob Nelson, President of POWER Retailing. I have a proven system I'd like to give to every retail business — who's looking to liquidate store inventory FAST.

I'm thrilled to reveal the path to retailers who have been enriched from our marketing tool chest... and produced unparalleled levels of cash and success.

For more than 30 years, in the United States and Canada, my retail consulting company has helped thousands of retailers increase sales and profits and experience extraordinary results.

Our goal is really very simple — To help YOU make money and succeed. Our specialty is helping retailers with powerful strategies and time-tested solutions to successfully close your business.

I know the dilemma of owning a retail store because I've been there. As a former owner, I understand the pain of retailers who are faced by hard work... long hours... and in most cases not enough money.

As you are reading this book, you're likely looking for the very best way to get out of the business, but aren't sure of the most profitable way to do it.

I'm going to give you new insights so you can learn how to get the profits you deserve. What's amazing, these are real "Game Changers" that have helped retailers just like you produce record-setting results.

Skills To Identify And Analyze

You'll reap the benefits to unlock and recover the wealth in your business, and it can be done faster and produce more money than selling your store as an ongoing business!

Closing your business is one of the most important single decisions that you will ever make. It requires specific details, a precise marketing system and highly strategic plan.

With expert advice and assistance, your business can be liquidated in six to eight weeks. And you will have the money up front — Cash you can take to the bank!

We'll help you quickly recognize and replace old, outdated methods with fresh merchandising and advertising techniques to bring immediate results.

When you apply our time-tested strategies you'll skyrocket your sales, slash advertising costs and attract crowds of eager customers to your store.

Best of all, our fee costs only a tiny fraction of the extra revenues we can help you produce.

Discover The Power Principles

No matter how many things you've tried before, with a proven track record our sure-fire system offers you the most profitable, exclusive and accelerated plans available.

It's the Ultimate System to maximize sales and profits. Whether you are a large or small business owner, there are amazing "Power Principles" and while each one has a dynamic value of its own, they have a common theme: They are all designed to put more cash in your pocket and bring more customers to your business!

Viewed as an industry leader, we've assisted in the disposal of inventories, helped stores close, retire, reorganize and merged stores, saved owners from bankruptcy, eliminated business debt, and optimized the value of assets available in every business.

So please read on...

Quickly Solve Your Biggest Challenge

Make A Successful Switch In Your Life

Finally, an affordable and profitable liquidation system designed just for your business!

Our passion is to help retailers just like you. After years of researching, testing, and applying the most effective retail strategies, we'll show you how to target your customers with the right message, in the right manner, and at the right time.

We'll make your registers ring with dozens of ways to give your business a superior advantage. With less worry and less risk, POWER Retailing's innovative techniques have helped thousands of established retail stores generate <u>tens-of-thousands of</u> <u>additional dollars</u> and get the biggest payback from their stock.

It's not easy running your own business. Most stores are just surviving while only a few actually earn big profits. As an accomplished retailer, you know from experience just getting customers to respond to your advertising effort is an enormous challenge.

Never Before Has It Been So Easy To Make Sales Surge!

When you hire Power Retailing, all you need is to apply the step-by-step plan and have the desire to succeed. We'll supply you with the rest.

We know you don't just want a bunch of old theories. What you want are solutions and clear-cut ideas to help unlock and recover the maximum value of your business assets. But there is more than that...

How would you like more than 50 powerful plans, exit strategies and advertising tools to immediately profit and sell your inventory with far less stress, effort and expense?

You will gain private access to our exclusive plans and coaching programs and the many options that apply to you:

> # Using POWER Retailing's system you can expect to recover up to 100% to 150% the cost of your inventory.

No Large Up-Front Fees!

We'll make your job easy and custom-tailor a plan with your approval and put all of the factors into action. Once the fundamental steps are applied and combined – you'll find that 200%, even 300% sales increases are typical results our clients get.

But You Will Never Experience A Dramatic Difference If You...

- Don't have the essential tools to take action.

- Don't do an exceptional job of motivating your customers to respond.

- Don't do the strongest job to sell them once you have their attention...

You are taking away the profits you could potentially be earning!

Getting just one of these sales-building techniques wrong can literally cost you thousands of dollars in lost profits or worse, put you further in debt.

- ✓ Do you have the business skills critical to your success?
- ✓ Are you adaptable to changing conditions?
- ✓ Do you have an effective strategy to attract customers and multiply sales?
- ✓ Can you take professional advice from others?

Is It TIME To Close Your Store?

Now You Can Write Your Own Ticket To Success

It's your passion. It's your livelihood. It's your business. In many ways, it's your life... and it may be time to sell it. You know how to run a business, but the skills and strategies needed to successfully close down your business is an entirely different animal.

In fact, there are proven, specific methods to close your business, and it can be very positive and highly PROFITABLE experience.

It's difficult for retailers who have had the same business for many years to change their thinking. Faced with slow sales, they keep spending money and energy on things that don't work anymore.

What Keeps You Up Most At Night?

Don't let emotions make business decisions. As you might expect, some people feel an attachment that allows things to get in the way of common sense.

Overwhelmed: The idea of selling your business has you tossing and turning at night. You don't even know where to begin.

Confused: Uneasy about the entire experience and perhaps already disillusioned by information you have gathered already.

Failure: You feel you could have done more to make your business more valuable or profitable.

Fear: You are fearful of making the wrong decisions and having to deal with a dire result and debt.

Skeptical: You doubt advice from industry experts.

Don't be too proud and fighting letting go. Closing your business does not mean failure; it is merely a part of the business life cycle.

If your store is caught between an inventory surplus and cash flow squeeze, and your life savings are tied to the business, you're not alone.

All kinds of retail businesses benefit from POWER Retailing's exit strategies and store closing plans – smart merchants who are ready to make a positive change and take the correct action.

Testimonials

What our customers say about closing vs. selling their business:

"By far, the best investment I have ever made. I have made so much more money doing my store closing sale than I could have EVER made selling my business. Thank you for ALL your help."
Kristen Oliver
San Angelo, Texas

Here is what John Schell had to say about the results of his Retirement Sale: *"Believe me, it's the only way to go. All cash. No carrying paper. We sold wall to wall and will net more money using POWER Retailing."*
John Schell
Denver, Colorado

At the end of Sharon Johnson's store closing sale, she said: *"Amazing! I did more in 8 weeks than I normally did in 6 months. I was able to realize enough income to pay off all debt and have a cushion for my future plans."*
Sharon Johnson
Mesa, Arizona

Break FREE From Frustration And Failure

Break Through The Barriers To Greater Profits And Success

The Internet And E-Commerce Are Changing The Rules Of Retailing!

There is a Specialty Store Revolution going on. Small and medium-sized stores are under attack and besieged with a wave of severe competition: Mobile devices are being used for online shopping, cyber discounts, price matching and free shipping.

Giants Rule Today's Marketplace. Internet businesses are blitzing from one side while Wal-Mart, retail outlets, and national discounters are sucking dollars from the other direction.

Why Smart Store Owners Turn To POWER Retailing

We Offer The Most Effective, Exclusive And Profitable Retail Liquidation Plans Available.

Highly successful retailers aren't any more talented, or intelligent than you. They simply have learned how to make money and do things in a different way. But most businesses don't know how to implement a strategic plan. **Do You?**

Business Today Is Tougher Than Ever Before!

Even in a slow economy, we have helped retail stores liquidate inventory, reorganize, remodel, relocate, retire, eliminate excessive debt, and optimize the value of hidden assets available in every business.

Are you looking for strategic techniques that work?

- Interested in doubling and tripling sales?

- Making enough money in your business?

- Feeling like you have tried everything and don't know what to do next?

- In need of an effective sales-driven plan to raise cash flow and pay off business debt?

- Interested in "trade secrets" to maximize your income, results and financial success?

Power Retailing uses the latest selling, marketing, advertising and social media tactics to drive more customers, make more money, and give more exposure to your sale.

With a keen understanding of the many challenges retailers face, our proven methods can be applied to virtually any type of retail store.

We'll help you:

1. Overcome your biggest challenge.

2. Use customer-winning strategies to get an overwhelming response.

3. Create a buying frenzy without contests or prizes.

4. Apply eye-catching ads and announcements that pull 500% better.

Every Business Needs A Comprehensive Plan

Unique Tools And Techniques To Make Your Store Money!

Our sure-fire plan is as essential for conducting a successful sale as having a blueprint for building a house; everything is designed to fit together like a puzzle. We'll show you how to do this and more.

Training and Direction

Qualified to give definitive and workable answers... there are no books, classrooms, colleges, or Internet resources to provide the essential marketing tools, ad layouts, custom signage, invaluable sales manual, and FREE consultation that you'll receive.

Most retailers are good at what they do...but they are not good at getting customers. They don't have the essential tools and specialized information to create the excitement to boost profits and make big things happen.

Does this sound familiar to you?

In an interview with <u>Nation's Business Magazine</u> relating to store owners, I stated this observation: *Retailers can do a lot of things right, but it doesn't matter what you do if you don't know how to get customers in the door.*

We'll help you focus on things that really matter!
- Increased Revenues
- Smaller Markdowns
- Higher Margins
- Lower Costs
- Greater Profits

Power Up Your Business

Overcome Your Fear and Nerves

We can help you prosper by redirecting your skills and marketing efforts in the right direction. People often ask the question: "Why can't I do this myself?"

Answer: Our promotions work better and faster! Without a well-organized marketing plan it is going to cost you more MONEY in mistakes and blunders as you try to fill-in-the-blanks on your own.

Case studies show the majority of retailers don't have a powerful exit strategy. Because they don't know the details, they simply get stuck and lose THOUSANDS of dollars of unsold fixtures, store equipment and leftover stock.

With a proven track record, POWER Retailing's approach takes the guesswork out of the equation.

Don't get caught with unsold fixtures and leftover stock. Our marketing components increase store traffic 3-5 times normal, and that enables you to generate more revenue and drive more customers to your store.

1. Proven marketing techniques to double and triple your sales.

2. Dynamic ads and social media formats customers can't refuse.

3. Visual techniques to keep products moving out the door.

4. Control and adjust your inventory mix.

Unlock The Hidden Wealth In Your Business

Retail Strategies That Bring Amazing Results!

Quickly Turn Your Inventory Into...

POWER Retailing is built for all the needs retailers want. Doing things that you've probably never done or thought about before, we can help multiply your sales and get the biggest payback from your stock.

Haven't you ever run an ad only to have it fail?

Does your advertising approach make money and produce the response that you're really after?

Are your marketing methods effective as you'd like them to be?

Your Business Can't Survive Without Customers And Cash Flow!

> You may be doing a lot of the right things, but if you're like most retailers you're not getting the results you want.

POWER Retailing's remarkable high impact system is so advanced and affordable it costs no more than a small fraction of what your sale can produce.

You'll have a step-by-step recipe for topics such as: pricing for profit, reducing costs, effective offers and turning your inventory into cash. We'll answer your questions... give you the crucial details... and supply the materials to help you achieve an unprecedented level of success!

You'll be able to:

- Simplify your efforts with specific details for planning, organizing, and pricing inventory.

- Boost your sales volume without sacrificing the prices of merchandise.

- Create the urgency and excitement of a high profit, fun-filled sales event.

Redirect Your Skills And Marketing Efforts

Make More Money And Draw Customers To Your Business!

Exclusive Plans And Coaching Programs

Just information alone is not enough. It's the indispensable tools and timely components to catapult sales.

A recent survey shows the industry has changed:

- Business is tougher and more competitive.

- Business is more stressful and less fun.

- People are pumping more money in their business than they are taking out.

You don't have to struggle anymore. Power Retailing provides long-term gains, not just quick fixes. We'll help you conduct an exciting sale better and faster than you ever thought possible.

1. Simple strategies to make sales and profits surge.

2. Winning solutions to put more money in your pocket and turn your inventory into CASH.

3. Crucial information to avoid the most common mistakes and advertising blunders.

4. Timely procedures that your staff and customers need to know.

5. Compelling advertising layouts and creative social media formats to cut budgets in half.

Wake Up Your Customers And Make Them Buy NOW!

Informative Strategies That Will Work For You

Well help you become an assertive marketer who seeks out prime customers instead of waiting for customers to come to you. You'll discover how to attract crowds of customers and gain the greatest competitive edge.

Because of the explosive growth of today's Internet, and national discounters, thousands of "main street" independent stores have taken a huge drop in sales. They just don't know where to turn or what to do.

Without a Plan-Of-Action you'll be driving your customers to the exits, leaving your business high and dry and literally letting dollars fly out the door.

POWER Retailing's retail liquidation plans generate higher sales and profits and can be applied to almost any type of storefront business.

Today, you are doing business like everyone else is and possibly putting in more money than you are taking out, and that doesn't do the trick.

Just ten years ago many companies that were on the Fortune 500 list have totally vanished – they were either absorbed, downsized, bankrupted, or closed.

Wall Street analysts are predicting the shift of dollars going from retail...to travel, entertainment, home improvement and shopping on the Internet. That's why, whether you're five or fifty years in business, you're going to face some crucial decisions.

Pile Up New Profits And Cash Flow!

Supercharge Your Sales To Get Great Results

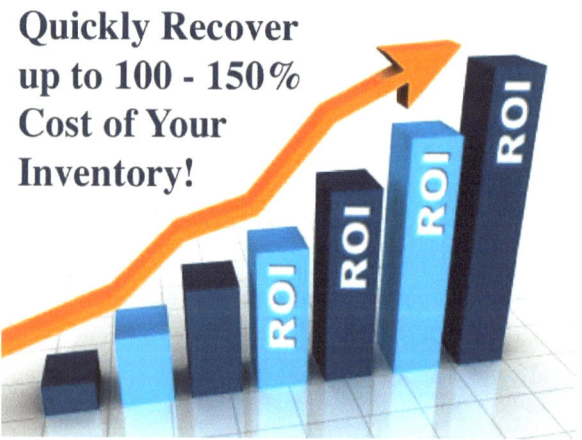

Quickly Recover up to 100 - 150% Cost of Your Inventory!

This totally integrated sales and marketing process can produce miracles for your business.

POWER Retailing's trade secrets are combinations of identifying, organizing and assembling:

- Powerful sales-building strategies, techniques and new breakthrough ideas.

- Proven formulas full of unique approaches and practical techniques for marketing, advertising, and merchandising.

The Ultimate Store Closing Plan!

We'll provide hands-on support and assistance to tailor everything to fit your image, products, size of business, customers and individual needs.

1. Guidelines, checklists and pricing charts to help you work smarter not harder.

2. The best ways to deal with your staff, landlords, and key store vendors.

3. Custom point-of-sale signs and eye-catching displays to organize and price merchandise.

4. How to plan, organize and control your sale with far less money, effort and expense.

5. How to build teamwork, maintain profit margins and sell out to the bare walls.

Avoid The Biggest Mistakes

Either You Get It, Or You Don't

It's what you don't know that you don't know!

Teamwork is the extra edge. Just because you're the boss doesn't mean you know everything and have the "know how" to solve every single challenge.

You're either someone who acts, and masterfully implements new breakthrough ideas to achieve the highest level of income and success – or you're not.

Do you wish you had the skills to motivate, persuade and influence customers to buy that you can use immediately? You can!

We'll show you dozens of sales-driven strategies and productivity-boosters to take action and keep your sales on track.

Do you recognize these 4 types of people?

1. The Know-It-All – They already have a fixed opinion on every issue.

2. The Passives – These people don't have good ideas and never take action.

3. The Gripers – Is anything ever right with them? They prefer complaining to finding solutions.

4. The "NO" People – They are quick to point out why something won't work.

What's worse, they are very skeptical people who sit on the sidelines and make...

The Biggest Marketing Mistakes

- DON'T know how to implement a strategic plan

- DON'T know how to start and when to finish

- DON'T have advertising techniques that work

- DON'T know how to get record-breaking results

- DON'T know how to get the highest dollar return

- DON'T know how to keep shoppers coming back

- DON'T know how to deal with store employees, creditors, landlords and key store vendors

Your Greatest Profit Center, Not Expense

What's In It For You?

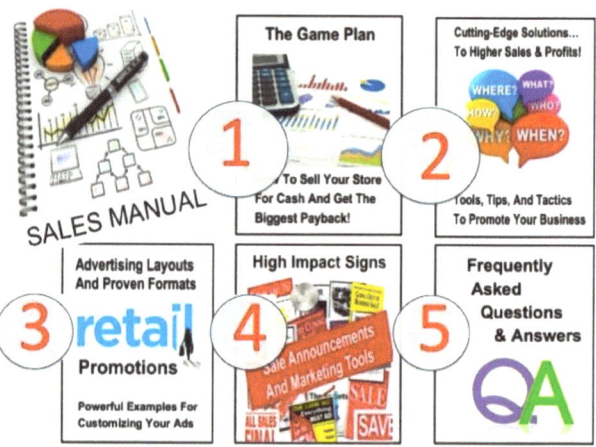

POWER Retailing's revolutionary system can bring you faster results and make you more money than any store auction, do-it-yourself sale, bulk sale, or other "exit strategies" will bring!

Whether you're a seasoned retailer or a marketing expert, we'll give you clear and specific advertising methods to out-sell, out-market and out-produce what you are doing now.

At a cost you can easily afford, we'll show you how to focus and get incredible results using the steps that make the difference between failure and success.

Rise To New Levels Of Business And Personal Success!

Once you apply our Strategic Formula For Success, the profitability of your customers' response, cash flow, advertising outcome, average order, frequency of purchases, and sales volume all go up. Not just in small steps, but by giant leaps!

Confidence-Builders To Meet Your Expectations

Testimonial...

"Power Retailing has guided me through one of the most difficult business transitions there are.

First, your voice and confidence calmed me down when I was paralyzed with fear. You gave me a heads up as to what to expect.

Had I not contacted Power Retailing, this would have been beyond awkward. I had so many questions. You explained to me, step-by-step, how to do this in a positive way.

As to the amount of sales -- I can pay my bills from only six business days! That was the point. I couldn't have done it without you."

Maggie Jackovitz - Lindale, TX

Open Your Mind To New Breakthrough Ideas

Practical Solutions For Retailers

Never has America's retail industry become so competitive and challenging!

Every business presents a unique set of conditions, challenges and goals. Liquidating your inventory demands change and understanding the dynamics of planning, advertising and promoting business.

To peak performance and get the best results, it is rare for one person to play all these roles equally well. You must know which parts you can handle and which parts you're going to need help with to attain your desired goal.

Succeeding In Today's Markets

THE BALTIMORE BUSINESS JOURNAL interviewed me about how small businesses can prepare for the battle against the bigger discount stores and mass merchandisers.

The news headline *"Stores Grid for the Superstore Invasion"* had the elements of a movie of invading Martians better known in the retail industry as... "The Category Killers."

As I mentioned during this interview: *There are solutions, but Category Killers are here to stay – you're going to have to deal with them. So many people are in denial and they think it's going to change, and it's not. Small stores have to make big changes if they want to survive.*

Isn't it sad that most retailers spend money on high rent, poor advertising and store overhead, but never take time to learn **"how to"** promote their business? It must seem so simple that people think they are already experts at it. Don't be the Lone Ranger...

- **Stop** being stuck with costs eating up your profits!
- **Stop** doing what's not working!
- **Stop** doing everything yourself!

Because the factors of a liquidation sale are different from any other event – it's all about **"know how"** and the tactical information to master an engaging money making sales event.

The Essential "Nuts And Bolts" You'd Better Know!

If you're looking for the right solution, don't risk another dime on things that don't work.

We'll give you FIVE precise steps to help unlock the wealth and overlooked opportunities in your business.

1) How to take action and initiate change.

2) How to create a comprehensive strategy.

3) How to skyrocket your sales and profits.

4) How to create customer urgency to buy NOW.

5) How to design a Sales And Marketing Plan that puts your store out in front of the pack.

Why Choose Us?

Turn Your Vision Into Reality!

Now you can get higher profits even if the economy remains slow!

POWER Retailing's team is here to help make your job easier and get to your goal faster...

We'll give you the tools... we'll give you the strategy and integrated plan... And we'll give you the training, direction, and attention to achieve your goal.

It is important to recognize and identify that what you don't know can end up costing you money, and reduce the chance of achieving success. Hiring an expert with specialized skills and knowledge can be the most profitable decision you can ever make.

Stop Worrying! POWER Retailing helps you prosper and replace outdated methods with new approaches to bring immediate results.

A proven Plan of Action with money making benefits

Turn obsolete inventory, old fixtures, and store equipment into cash

Market, advertise, and promote your sale at the lowest cost

Sell your inventory fast without sacrificing it

Attract crowds of buyers and get an overwhelming response

Know when to take markdowns and not get caught with leftover stock

---

How Does It Work?

We'll Make Your Cash Registers Ring!

With rising costs and stagnant revenues, are you caught between an inventory surplus and cash flow squeeze – not knowing what to do?

We'll show you the most accelerated and prosperous ways to increase sales and how to avoid the most common mistakes. Much of these sales-building concepts are virtually unknown by most retailers.

To catapult customer traffic and sales, we'll show you how to set your store apart from the competition by applying a jam-packed marketing "tool chest" of fresh ideas and advertising strategies to drive it all.

Implementation Is Everything!

- Imagine - Having a plan to ensure success

- Imagine - Relieving frustration and stress

- Imagine - Reducing excessive debt

- Imagine - Recouping capital in your inventory

- Imagine - the advantage of having your own business consultant that is a tax deduction

You'll have clear-cut steps, practical answers, new ideas and approaches from the services we provide.

- Identify Problems: to provide practical answers with workable solutions.

- Objectivity: to implement fresh ideas with an impartial viewpoint.

- Sales Expertise: to offer advice and assistance to get superior results.

The Fast Path To Success

Focus On Your Objectives

Wouldn't you like time-tested strategies and cash flow solutions to immediately profit during these fast-changing times?

- Increased revenues

- Smaller markdowns

- Higher margins

- Lower costs

- Greater profits

Power Retailing's strategies have caught the attention of Kenneth E. Stone, Ph. D., Professor of Economics at Iowa State University.

Dr. Stone commented, **"Power Retailing doesn't offer theories, it offers proven formulas for success."**

Solutions Rather Than Just Advice

Retailers All Over America Rely On Our Power Principles

The secret to higher sales and profits is simply using the right tools. Stores wedded to the same old way of doing things are almost sure to fail. Most business owners can be divided into two main categories:

- Those who resist change!
- Those who welcome change!

Our clients are business people who not only welcome change – but they are ready for change!

National chains and types of stores we work with:

Women's Apparel... Men's Apparel... Children's stores... Toy... Hunting and Fishing... Sporting Goods... Gift and Card Stores... Shoe Stores... Stationery... Book Stores... Home Décor... Pet Stores... Teacher Supplies... Video... Furniture... Garden and Statuary... Costume and Magic... Scrapbook... Golf... Dance... Hobby... Lighting... Art... Wedding and Bridal... Western... Antique... Health... Luggage... Fabric/Quilting and more.

Learn how to take control of your business. With less time, money, and expense you'll have new ideas, trade secrets, specific details and dozens of things that you've never done or thought about before.

Ask yourself these questions...

☑ Has the time come to quit or retire from your business?

☑ Are you worried about the direction where your business is headed?

☑ Do you feel stress and frustrated because you are not making enough money?

☑ Is all of your working capital and life savings tied up in your inventory?

☑ Are you borrowing more money than you can pay back from profits?

☑ Are you concerned about generating enough cash to pay current debts?

If your answer is "YES" to any of the above questions and need a solution, it's time for us to meet. Let us help you make the most of every obstacle you face.

Discover Your Options

Exit Strategies, Liquidation And Cash Flow Plans

Whether you want to downsize, sell your store, retire, liquidate inventory, or successfully go out of business, we can solve your most pressing problem and get the biggest payback from your stock.

Not only do we provide a strategic "game plan" that will produce immediate financial benefits, we also provide the materials and ongoing support you need.

If you are seeking advice from family and friends, beware. Remember: it is not their money or their problem and they don't admit they don't have a well-organized strategic marketing plan that you can use.

Discover the Secrets of...

Right from the start, you'll have "State-of-the-art" strategies that you can apply NOW. We'll help you watch every penny you spend and make sure every dollar provides a significant and quick return.

We respect your image and reputation and make certain that our advice and assistance is private, practical, and completely understood.

OPTION 1) Expert On-Site Implementation and In-Store Consultation

OPTION 2) Comprehensive Store Closing Tool Kit and Ongoing Consultation

Our FREE consultation is strictly 100% confidential.

Because every store is unique and presents different challenges and goals, we customize everything to fit your customers, products, budgets, and goals.

The rewards can be amazing if you let POWER Retailing do the hard work for you. If our strategic plan is not all that we have presented it to be, and if you aren't thrilled with the customers' response, cash flow and revenues your sale produces, we will do everything to make it right and help you succeed!

Do Your Sale With Confidence!

Throughout the years, we've helped stores produce millions of additional dollars and not get caught with store fixtures, equipment, and leftover stock.

We'll make the job easy and save you thousands of dollars to sell, advertise and promote your business at the lowest possible cost. **We Guarantee It.**

You'll have dozens of customer-winning strategies, superior advertising tools, and combinations of marketing techniques to easily set up, conduct and launch a successful Store Closing Sales Event.

With workable solutions and not just advice, you'll immediately gain considerable benefits without the hassle, inconvenience and marketing expense.

Success Stories
& Testimonials

"I am very pleased with the results of the sale. The sale worked so quickly that I was out of stock a week before the anticipated closing. I have paid all the bills and have money left over.

I absolutely could not have done it without POWER Retailing's help. It was great to relax and just follow the instructions I received. The impact of the signage got my customers attention and kept them buying.

It was an excellent investment. As a small business owner I have learned to turn to the experts to be successful. POWER Retailing gave me the skills I needed to successfully liquidate."

Ellen Graves - Albany, CA

After 12 successful years in business and recognized as the Number One Scrapbook Store in the State of Kansas, Bob and Kathy decided to call it quits and used POWER Retailing's Store Closing System.

Implementing a comprehensive Game Plan to make sales soar, before the store opened excited customers were lined up at their door...

Starting with $190,000 inventory at cost, daily sales shot up five times normal and produced $337,155 dollars including fixtures. This 5 week sale made a profit of $147,155 dollars.

Bob and Kathy said: "We did not want to sign a new lease and it is time to move on and recover our assets."

After 20 successful years, Kristen Oliver the owner of Sugar Baker's Kitchen Emporium in San Angelo, Texas turned to POWER Retailing to help launch her Store Closing Sale.

Kristen said: "Well, you were right it was insanity. The first day ended up doing $28,141 after tax. This sale has blown us away how successful it has been...

Absolutely the best investment I have ever made. You led me step-by-step how to close the store with the greatest return and I couldn't be more pleased with the results.

I was hoping to close in 10 weeks and it looks like it will take five at the most. I have made so much more money doing my Store Closing Sale than I could have ever received trying to sell my business!"

For 46 years, Terry Brady owned a popular Hunting and Fishing Store in Montana. Employing POWER Retailing's system, we worked with Terry to launch his Store Wide Retirement Sale.

Carefully planned, organized, and set up to liquidate $1 Million dollars of inventory, with a loyal customer following, shoppers lined up at store counters with their arms filled with hunting, fishing, and camping supplies...

Realizing immediate pay-offs and benefits, Terry was proud to say: "The Opening Day of my action-packed sale produced $175,000 dollars."

Designed to fit the inventory mix and size of stock, Terry Brady's sale turned out to be an exciting sales event that his customers will never forget.

After 12 years in business, Mrs. Connie Barr, owner of Magical Creations, a ladies' apparel and gift store in Portland, Oregon, utilized our Store Closing Plan.

Generating a large cash flow, POWER Retailing stopped the financial drain on the business assets.

Surprised by the final results, Connie Barr said: "We did far better than any of my friends that had stores around the country and were left with huge debt they will be facing for the rest of their lives.

Selling our inventory and store fixtures faster than expected, we ended up without any debt. We felt it was a huge success!

I want to thank you for your part in getting us through that."

Bob and Jessie Adams, owned a well-established 34-year Toy and Game Store in Twin Falls, Idaho. Because of the economy and their contract was up, this family owned business hired POWER Retailing to maximize sales and increase bottom-line profits.

Using POWER Retailing's Store Closing Plan and Formula for Success, Bob Adams said: "Having a plan relieves a lot of stress and tension. There is more relaxation about it and we are not pressed."

Mrs. Jessie Adams acknowledged: "It's just amazing. As a business owner the one thing we didn't have a clue about was how to shut it down."

During the initial hours of the sale, Jessie Adams added: "We're really impressed. Lots of people here, everyone is buying and armloads of products are going to the front counter... Oh it's fabulous."

Mr. Tim Heffley, of Sharps Ace Hardware located in Hemet, California, was known as the proud owner of a well-established hardware store in town.

Because of "Big Box" discounters coming to town, Tim was concerned about the severe competition and future of his business.

With a blockbuster sale that got tremendous results, Tim said: "POWER Retailing definitely got my sale off and running; 14 days into the sale, I sold 82.5% of my inventory at cost.

I started with approx. 100k of store inventory and have generated $82,562.53 in sales. I was hoping for 70-75% for the entire event."

Attracting crowds of customers and quickly turning merchandise into cash, Tim acknowledged: "With your excellent help, I sold my inventory and store fixtures to the bare walls in just 21 days."

A Company With More Than 30 Years Experience

Leadership, Teamwork, Execution

YOU'LL EVER MAKE

Learn how over 30 years of experience assures more money for you! Our proven strategies and exclusive marketing plans mean faster results – and more cash flow than with any other company at any price!

Don't sacrifice your merchandise! Through coaching and hands-on consultation, we'll give you new ideas, specific details, proven advertising tools, plus dozens of ways to create customer urgency and excitement – that you've never done or thought about before.

How Do We Help You?

It's simple. We don't waste your time with vague theories or irrelevant concepts. We focus on practical, how-to information you can put to use right away. That means tools, tips and techniques that have an instant impact on your effectiveness.

Step-by-step checklists and powerful **"extras"** to redirect your efforts in the right direction:

1. Designed to deliver amazing results and make profits soar, our plans provide massive benefits and substantial returns for every penny you spend.

2. You'll receive expert consultation and FREE sales support. Plus an invaluable sales manual filled with detailed information and procedures you'll use again and again.

3. From start to finish, you'll be able to save loads of hassle and rewarding yourself for all of your efforts. Best of all, you'll have all the money up front...Cash you can take to the bank.

Marketing, Advertising and Promoting Your Sale!

So how do you put on a successful liquidation, store closing, retirement, or going out of business sale? The most important requirement is an integrated, step-by-step marketing plan.

Focus on the best months for store traffic. Once you decide when to start your sale, you should allow 3 to 4 weeks for preparation.

Your main concern is to turn inventory into cash. With careful planning you'll be able to insure higher sales and profits by preparing effective advertising and balancing store inventory.

Ads can be placed and changed on relatively short notice allowing you to design last-minute revisions as your sale goes through its different phases. You can adjust prices, percentages, selections, and other special points as the sale continues.

To receive optimal response, consider the appeal of your message, and its sense of urgency. Ads should be easily recognizable with a dominant headline clearly stating percentages or ranges of prices to create customer urgency.

The objective of advertising is to sell! Its purpose is to bring more customers into your store. A good ad can run over and over again, until you become bored with it. It can also be reprinted and used as fliers, hand-outs, mailers or even enlarged and used as a poster.

Once your store is set up, all signs and banners are put into place and merchandise is priced, your store will appear to be different. This is what creates the compelling presentation, buying urgency and customer excitement for your sale. Pay attention to details:

- Prepare to have enough staff.
- Watch for slow-moving categories.
- Change displays if there seems to be little interest.
- Products must be accessible to see, touch, and smell.
- Arrange merchandise by size, type and categories.

If you need to buy additional merchandise for the sale, keep this in mind: the first week will have the largest customer impact. These are the "Big Volume Days," so be sure your store is fully stocked for the opening.

Don't be too proud to ask for help, we all need help sometimes. It is important to recognize that what you don't know can end up costing you tons of money, hurt the odds of success, and reduce the chance of achieving your goals.

As well-qualified consultants, our function is to provide the easiest, quickest and safest solution to solve your inventory or cash flow problems to promptly eliminate stress, fear or pain and achieve the results you've been looking for – and so much more!

Hiring an expert with specialized skills and years of experience can be the most profitable decision you'll ever make. You're either someone who acts and wants to apply new ways to succeed – OR YOU'RE NOT.

Designed to deliver fresh insights and opportunities, we can be your greatest profit center, not an expense!

DON'T WAIT!
CALL TODAY
480-460-1980

Pinpoint Your Concerns

Are You Planning To Close, Or Just Need Cash In Your Business?

Ask Yourself These Questions...

1. Looking For Answers?

2. Have Few Or No Options?

3. Need A Solution RIGHT NOW?

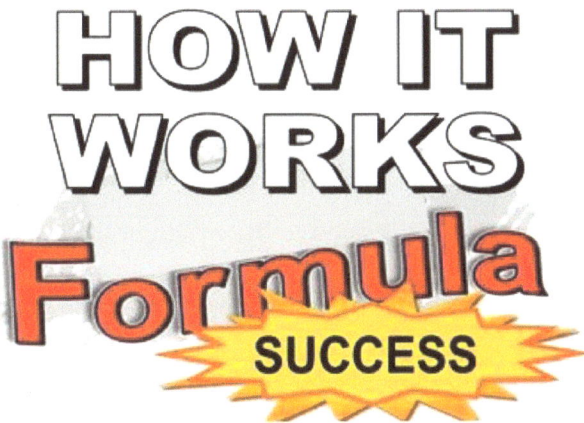

What you get to sell your inventory and achieve your Goals.

Discover "trade secrets" to out-sell, out-market, and out-produce your competition.

POWER Retailing's strategies and exclusive advertising tools mean faster results and more cash flow than with any other company at any price!

THE GOOD NEWS
Keeps Getting Better!

No Large Up-Front Fees!

POWER Retailing will make you more money far above and beyond what any other inventory auction, or do-it-yourself plan will bring.

Viewed as leading experts in the USA and Canada our innovative strategy has increased bottom line profits for thousands of retailers – and we can do the same for YOU!

With a rich history of success, we'll give you a proven "game plan" to instantly increase your sales.

The results and financial benefits can be amazing if you let POWER Retailing do the hard work for you.

Just take a look at
EVERYTHING you get...

Steps To Success!

√ How to solve your biggest business challenge.

√ Customer-winning techniques to double and triple your sales.

√ Save money without contests or giving away expensive prizes.

√ Exciting layouts and social media formats to advertise your sale.

√ Sales-driven strategies to produce record-breaking sales.

√ Powerful advertising tools and techniques – you can use Now.

√ Proven ways to drive traffic and new customers to your store.

√ Custom-designed signs and eye-catching displays to boost sales.

√ Time-tested tactics to promote your sale at the lowest possible cost.

√ How to sell obsolete merchandise that no one seems to want.

√ How to increase purchases and keep your customers coming back.

√ How to generate store traffic and sell everything to the bare walls.

√ How to replace outdated methods with new Ads that pull 500% better.

√ Guidelines and checklists to help you work smarter, not harder.

√ How to target customers and the best type of advertising to use.

√ Ideas to instantly boost profits and put money in your bank account.

√ Compelling point-of-sale and attention-getting displays to create impact.

√ Special Social Media, Facebook and E-mail announcements to use.

√ Preferred "customer invitations" to get an overwhelming response.

√ Advertising layouts and proven formats to cut your budget in half.

√ Steps to avoid marketing mistakes and advertising blunders.

√ Simple techniques to increase profits and make sales surge.

√ When to take markdowns during the entire process of the sale.

√ How to solve financial challenges and eliminate excessive debt.

√ How to break the NEWS to your staff, customers, and vendors.

√ The secret "nuts and bolts" to get the highest possible dollar return.

√ How to build teamwork, keep your employees and get their support.

√ The best way to deal with landlords, banks and key store vendors.

√ How to eliminate frustration and fear and turn your vision into reality...

Best of all, you'll have a sure-fire plan to quickly and safely recover 100% – 150% the cost of inventory.

The secret to success is having the right tools to do the job. If you are working more and enjoying it less, we can make a successful switch in your life...

Most importantly, you'll have Free 24/7 marketing and advertising support – and gain private access to our exclusive plans and hands-on coaching programs.

Notes

Notes

www.ingramcontent.com/pod-product-compliance
Lightning Source LLC
Chambersburg PA
CBHW040836180526
45159CB00001B/212